UNDERSTANDING THE BILL OF RIGHTS

WRITTEN BY SALLY SENZELL ISAACS

Published in 2014 by Bendon Publishing International, Inc.
All rights reserved. Printed in the U.S.A.

The BENDON name and logo are trademarks of Bendon Publishing International, Inc.
Ashland, OH 44805 • 1-888-5-BENDON
bendonpub.com

LEVEL **3** READER

GRADES 2 TO 4 · READING LEVEL

Originally produced for Crabtree Publishing Company by Bender Richardson White, U.K.
Editor-in-Chief: Lionel Bender; Editor: Kelley MacAulay; Consultant: Professor Richard Jensen
Photographs: © Corbis: Bettman: p. 22, 24; Bob Krist: p. 16
© Northwind Picture Archives: cover, p. 4, 5, 6, 7, 9, 10, 11, 12, 14, 15, 17, 18, 21
© Shutterstock.com: p: 2, 13, 19, 23
© The Granger Collection: p. 8
© Wikipedia.com: cover (background)

OUR CONSTITUTION

The United States Constitution is a written plan or set of rules for the national government. It explains how laws are made, how leaders are chosen, and what the national government can and cannot do.

The Constitution includes ten additions called amendments. These ten amendments are the Bill of Rights. They give the American people important rights and freedoms.

◀ *The Constitution was approved by the national government in 1788. The Bill of Rights became part of the Constitution three years later, in 1791.*

THE BILL OF RIGHTS: TEN AMENDMENTS

First   Freedom of religion, speech, the press, assembly (meeting), and petition (demanding change)

Second   The right to bear arms (guns)

Third   During peacetime, citizens cannot be forced to feed and house soldiers

Fourth   People and homes cannot be searched without a good reason

Fifth   People accused of crimes must be treated fairly

Sixth   The right to a speedy, public, and fair trial

Seventh   The right to a jury trial

Eighth   Punishment may not be cruel and unusual

Ninth   Americans have other rights, even if they are not listed in the Bill of Rights. As questions arise, judges will decide about other rights

Tenth   The U.S. government has only the powers listed in the Constitution

The Bill of Rights was created at a time when the United States had only recently been formed. Before this time, people in America were not always free to say and do as they wished or to follow their religious beliefs. Some people were sent to jail without first having a fair trial. The Bill of Rights provided Americans with certain freedoms that cannot be taken away.

The First Congress

Before the United States became a nation, it was 13 colonies ruled by Britain. Colonists had to follow Britain's laws and pay taxes to Britain. A tax is money that people pay to the government to run a country. By 1765, colonists were angry with Britain. Britain's government kept adding new taxes. Every time the colonists bought such items as newspapers, cloth, sugar, or tea, they had to pay extra money to Britain.

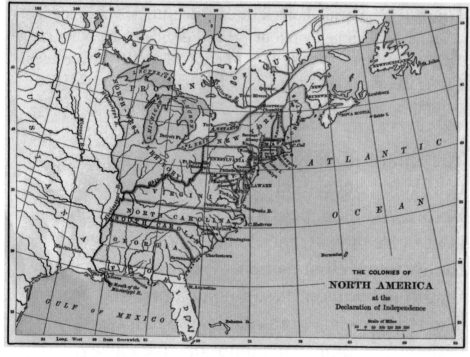

▲ *A map of the 13 American colonies and territory*

◀ *Colonial leaders met in houses and taverns to make plans for the Congress.*

In 1774, leaders from the colonies held a meeting in Philadelphia called the Continental Congress. Each colony sent representatives. A representative is someone who speaks for other people. At the meeting, the representatives discussed their problems with Britain.

Britain's King George III heard about the Continental Congress. He wondered how the colonists could turn against their country. He sent soldiers to the colonies to keep the colonists under control. The king created laws that forced the colonists to house British soldiers. Then the king told the colonists to stop having meetings about Britain's rule. The colonists refused to stop and held their meetings secretly.

REVOLUTION!

In April 1775, about 700 British soldiers headed to the towns of Lexington and Concord in Massachusetts. They had heard that colonial soldiers there were collecting guns. When the armed colonists met the British soldiers, a battle broke out between them. This was the first battle in the American Revolution. A revolution is a strong action by people to change their government. The American Revolution lasted for six years. The colonists who fought for their independence from Britain were called Patriots.

▲ *Paul Revere warned the colonists in Massachusetts.*

Messages on horseback

The colonists in Lexington were ready to protect themselves against the British soldiers. They had been warned by Paul Revere and William Dawes that soldiers were on their way. The two men had ridden through the town shouting, "The British are coming!"

INDEPENDENCE

While the Patriots and the British were at war, leaders from the colonies continued to meet. They planned the Declaration of Independence to announce that the colonies would separate from Britain and create their own government and laws.

Thomas Jefferson wrote the Declaration of Independence. In it he wrote that people are born with rights that a government cannot take away. These include the rights to "*life, liberty, and the pursuit of happiness.*" Liberty means freedom. The Declaration also said that "*all men are created equal.*" This means that no one person should have more rights than another.

▲ *Thomas Jefferson wrote the Declaration of Independence.*

On July 4, 1776, Congress voted "yes" to accept the Declaration of Independence. In 1781, the Patriots won the American Revolution. The 13 colonies became 13 states, and the United States of America was born.

A NEW GOVERNMENT

In planning for the new national government, the leaders of the states asked that most of the power remain with the state governments. The first plan for the national government was called the Articles of Confederation. Congress accepted this plan in 1777.

The United States had many problems under the Articles. The national government needed money, but only the states could collect taxes. The states often refused to give tax money to the national government. The states acted like separate countries.

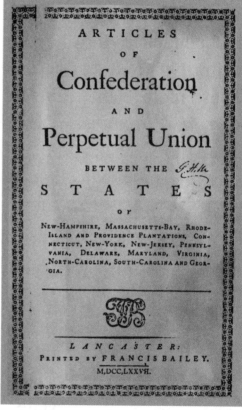

▲ *The Articles of Confederation*

A NEW PLAN

In 1787, state representatives met again to write a new plan for the national government. The meeting was called the Constitutional Convention. The leaders chose General George Washington to be president of the meeting. The new plan was called the United States Constitution. The Constitution gave more power to the national government and less to the states.

▼ *The United States Constitution was signed by Congress on September 17, 1787.*

THE CONSTITUTION

The Constitution explains that there are three branches of government. The legislative branch makes the laws. It includes two houses of Congress: the House of Representatives and the Senate. The executive branch is led by the President and makes sure that the laws are carried out. The judicial branch is made of courts and judges. They interpret, or explain, the laws.

Branches of government

Legislative Branch
Congress:
1. Senate
2. House of Representatives

Executive Branch
Led by the President

Judicial Branch
Courts and judges

▲ *James Madison wrote many parts of the Constitution.*

Lessons from history

Some of James Madison's ideas for the Constitution came from Britain's Magna Carta. In 1215, people in Britain gathered together and forced their king, John, to sign this document. The Magna Carta took some powers from the king and gave them to the people.

▶ *King John signing the Magna Carta*

FOR OR AGAINST?

After the Constitution was written, the states had to approve it. Americans who wanted the Constitution were called Federalists. Those who did not want it were called Anti-Federalists. Anti-Federalists were afraid that, under the Constitution, the national government would be too powerful and could take rights away from people. In the end, all 13 states voted "yes" to the Constitution. Many of them asked for something in return, however. They wanted to add a Bill of Rights. This addition would protect the people from the government.

THE BILL OF RIGHTS

On December 15, 1792, four years after the Constitution had been signed, ten amendments were added to the Constitution. This was called the Bill of Rights. It lists freedoms that all Americans have. It says that the government cannot stop Americans from enjoying these freedoms unless the government has a very good reason.

◀ *George Washington was made the first U.S. President in 1789. Every President must promise to* "preserve, protect, and defend the Constitution of the United States."

Freedom of Speech

The leaders who wrote the Bill of Rights disliked how British soldiers had arrested people who spoke against King George III. They remembered how the king had made the colonists stop having meetings. The First Amendment ensured that this would never happen again in the United States. This amendment says that Americans can share their beliefs, no matter what those beliefs are. Americans can have meetings, give speeches, carry signs, write stories, and sing songs about anything they want.

▼ *Americans can speak freely, even if other people disagree.*

FREEDOM OF THE PRESS

In 1734, John Peter Zenger was a local newspaper printer in the colony of New York. Some of his stories criticized the colony's British governor. The stories said that the governor was unfair to colonists. The governor arrested Zenger and sent him to jail.

The next year, John Peter Zenger was put on trial so that a jury of citizens could decide if he deserved to be in jail. The jury, guided by a judge, decided that Zenger should be freed. They felt he should be allowed to print whatever he wanted, as long as it was true.

▶ *Colonists read reports and stories printed in the newspapers. The newspapers were sold in shops.*

▲ *John Peter Zenger was tried in a court before a judge and jury.*

When it was time to write the Bill of Rights, Americans remembered this trial and wanted to add freedom of the press as an amendment. The "press" now includes anything that people use to report the news, such as the radio, TV, newspapers, and the internet. In many countries, the government stops the news from being reported. The Bill of Rights does not allow this in the United States.

FREEDOM OF RELIGION

The First Amendment also promises freedom of religion. This allows Americans to believe and worship in any religion, or none at all. It also says that the United States government cannot support any one religion. In 1776, Britain supported a religion called the Church of England. The king was the head of the church. People who did not belong to this religion could lose their jobs or homes, or be put in jail.

▲ *Jewish people built this synagogue in Newport, Rhode Island, in 1763. It was the first synagogue in the United States.*

IT SHALL NOT HAPPEN AGAIN

Many people had moved to the American colonies because they wanted freedom of religion. They did not have this in Britain. However, in the early days of the colonies, some people were punished for their religious beliefs. Freedom of religion was added to the Bill of Rights to stop such things from happening.

Banished!
In 1637, a woman named Anne Hutchinson was leader of the Puritan religion in Massachusetts. Some of her beliefs were different from the other Puritans'. Massachusetts leaders forced Anne Hutchison out of the colony because of her different beliefs.

SELF PROTECTION

The Second Amendment says that people have the right *"to keep and bear arms."* This means that citizens who behave well can keep guns at home to protect themselves. During the American Revolution, Patriots had wanted to protect themselves from British soldiers. They had also wanted to be able to protect themselves from their national leaders if these people became unfair.

◄ *Patriot soldiers used their own guns to fight the British.*

Privacy

The Third Amendment of the Bill of Rights ensures that the government cannot force people to allow soldiers to live in their houses, as the British had done to the colonists. The Fourth Amendment gives Americans rights to privacy. For example, the police may not search a person's property unless there is a good reason to believe the person has committed a crime. The police must prove to a judge why the search should take place.

▲ *A police officer can ask to search a person's car if he or she thinks there is stolen or illegal property or criminal evidence in the vehicle.*

A Fair Trial

Police officers arrest criminals to keep our communities safe. However, Americans cannot be punished for crimes without fair trials. The Fifth, Sixth, Seventh, and Eighth Amendments of the Bill of Rights protect people who are accused of crimes.

**Some of the protections
for people accused of crimes**

- People must be told what they are accused of, such as theft, fraud, or murder.
- A jury of people from the same state must decide if a person is guilty or not.
- A person has the right to remain silent. This means the person does not have to answer questions that might lead the jury to think he or she is guilty of a crime.

- A trial must be "speedy" and open to the public.
- People have a right to get advice from a lawyer or have a lawyer speak for them.
- If a person is found guilty, their punishment cannot be cruel and unusual.
- If a person is found "not guilty," he or she cannot be tried again for the same crime.

◄ *For punishment, this man's feet are locked in place. He must sit in public for many days. Today, this punishment is not allowed because it is cruel.*

▼ *In a trial, a jury listens to both sides. The people of the jury decide if the accused person is guilty or not.*

LIMITING POWER

The first eight amendments of the Bill of Rights list the rights that Americans will always have. The Ninth Amendment says that just because other rights are not named in the Constitution does not mean these rights can be denied to the people. For example, people have the right to travel freely between the states. The Tenth Amendment stops the national government from taking on more powers than those that are listed in the Constitution.

▼ *You can see the Declaration of Independence, the Constitution, and the Bill of Rights in the National Archives in Washington, D.C.*

SEEKING JUSTICE

Sometimes, people think their rights have been violated. For example, people may say they have been denied freedom of speech. These people go to court to ask a judge or jury to decide if their treatment goes against the Bill of Rights. If people do not agree with a court's decision, they may take it to a higher court. The Supreme Court, the nation's highest court, has made many decisions about whether or not the Bill of Rights has been upheld.

▼ *The nine justices (judges) of the Supreme Court meet in this building in Washington, D.C.*

Still Growing

The first ten amendments were an important addition to the Constitution. Other amendments were added over the years. Some new amendments caused important changes in the United States. In 1865, the Thirteenth Amendment ended slavery. In 1920, the Nineteenth Amendment gave women the right to vote. More than 9,000 amendments have been proposed to Congress, but only 27 have been added to the Constitution.

Since the Constitution was signed, the nation has grown from 13 to 50 states. For more than 225 years, the Constitution has guided the United States government, and the Bill of Rights has protected its citizens.

▶ Members of the Senate vote on new amendments to the Bill of Rights.